The Armored Mind

Breaking Strongholds over the Mind

Concepts Geared for Spiritual and Mental Health

APOSTLE DR. SANDRA MITCHELL

ASN, BMin, M.Th., D.Div.

 FriesenPress

One Printers Way
Altona, MB R0G 0B0
Canada

www.friesenpress.com

Copyright © 2022 by Apostle Dr. Sandra Mitchell
First Edition — 2022

Photographers: Jonathan Mitchell and Deborah Mitchell
Design: David Mitchell
Pictures used in the book were purchased from Shutterstock.

ISBN
978-1-03-912724-1 (Hardcover)
978-1-03-912723-4 (Paperback)
978-1-03-912725-8 (eBook)

1. Body, Mind & Spirit, Healing, Prayer & Spiritual

Distributed to the trade by The Ingram Book Company

TABLE OF CONTENTS

APOSTLE DR. SANDRA MITCHELL

This book is dedicated to my late husband, Apostle Dr. Ernest Mortimer Mitchell (1937–2019), for his strength, love, and encouragement to me while he was alive.

To our children: Alison, Tasha, Kory, Richard, Jonathan and Allie, Abraham and Ledalis, Deborah, Jeremiah, Esther, and David.

To our grandchildren: Joshua, Nathan, Ariel, Noah, Avey, Jamill, Karelis, Kailani. Also, to all my family members. Especially, my sister, Rev. M. Grace Kelly, and my friend Lisa Porter, for being a source of encouragement to me. You are the "apple of my eye."

In memory of my sister, the late Apostle Elect Jenalfer Kelly (1958–2021). You will always be remembered for your faithfulness to the Lord, and to me as your Apostle.

Our Daystar friends and family from Daystar Ministries of Fort Lauderdale, Inc, Dba Daystar Connect and Fountain of Life—Apostle Dr. Sherron Parrish. Also, the various churches and leaders that patronizes Freedom Reigns Global Restoration Annual Convention. I love and appreciate you all very much. Continue to stay prayerful and connected!

Most of all, my sincere love and adoration to God my Heavenly Father and Friend, Jesus my Savior and Lord, and my Counselor and Guide the Holy Spirit.

INTRODUCTION

Anatomy is defined as a study of the structure or internal workings of something. It is also the branch of science concerned with the bodily structure of humans, animals, and other living organisms, especially as revealed by dissection and the separation of parts.

The mind is intangible, in that it cannot be defined by shape or size. The approach of this book, however, will involve some dissecting and separation of the mental processes, to better understand the structure or internal workings of the mind.

The question is often asked, "What is the difference between the mind and the brain?" For one, the brain is an organ, and the mind is not. It is believed that the brain is the physical place where the mind resides. This intangible system, so to speak, is the mastermind behind the whole operation of a person. The brain plays a central role in the control of most bodily functions, including awareness, movement, sensations, thoughts, speech, and memory. The mind also has a great influence in each of these areas as well. It is often referred to as "the thought processes of reason."

The spinal cord is connected to the section of the brain called the brain stem. Together they make up what is called the central nervous system. The spinal cord carries messages back and forth between the brain and the peripheral nerves. The peripheral nervous system is the second of two components of the nervous system. Its job is to dispatch data gathered by the body's sensory receptors to the central nervous system as quickly as possible to determine action.

Clear communication is seen as a vital role for the body's equilibrium. In the same manner, it becomes necessary for the mind to receive wisdom or counsel from its life-giving source (God) to exercise good judgment to make informed decisions. These decisions will affect not just physical well-being but also spiritual well-being. What the brain is to the body, the Spirit of the Lord is to the mind.

The armored mind will deal with mental processing on a physical and spiritual level. Understanding the anatomy of the mind will put one in the driver's seat to make those informed decisions. In so doing, it will foster more harmonious relationships—physical, emotional, and spiritual. The saying "the mind is a terrible thing to waste" is an inspired thought.

Not just for the acquiring of knowledge, but for the understanding of one's purpose for being.

The armored mind is revolutionary! Understanding the workings of the mind is the central theme of this book. This will be achieved by dissecting, separating, and administering remedies to its internal parts by the divine inspiration of the Holy Spirit. Breaking strongholds over the mind will help to accomplish this purpose, as set forth in this biological and spiritual approach to the mind. Let's get started on this quest for the spiritual and mental health of humanity!

This is a must-read book. Apostle Sandra Mitchell has been gifted with wisdom in this book to break strongholds from cultural, mental, physical, and spiritual realms. This book is filled with strategies that will equip and enable the believer with insights that will unlock the power to prevail over false images of the mind. Get ready for your mind to be made whole, healthy, and happy as you become Activated in this Present Truth!

-Apostle Anthony J. Hatcher
Bishop, Senior Pastor
Faith Life Outreach Christian Kathedral

1

BREAKING STRONGHOLDS OVER THE MIND

Understanding your personal warfare and why things are happening the way they are is the initial stage of breakthrough. Judges 4:1 state, "Again the Israelites did evil in the eyes of the Lord, now that Ehud was dead."[1] It is said that sometimes our good behavior will only last when the leader is in our presence. God expects his people not to be people pleasers, but rather God pleasers. As a result, Israel was in bondage and was cruelly oppressed by Jabin, king of Canaan. For twenty years they cried out to the Lord.[2]

God responded by having Deborah, the current judge in Israel, give a prophetic word to Barack, son of Abinoam, to go up against Sisera, commander of Jabin's army. Out of fear, Barack frankly told

Deborah that he would not go unless she joined him in battle. Even though Deborah decided to go with him, she told him that the honor would go to another because of the course that he was taking.[3] It was well-known that Jabin had 900 chariots of iron—a military outfit that far outnumbered the 10,000 men of Naphtali and Zebulun that he was to lead into battle. There was enough evidence in the natural for Barack to be afraid by human standards. However, he was more concerned with the number of chariots and horses than he was in trusting in the Name of the Lord! He had no faith in himself or the God of Heaven. He wore physical armor to battle, but his mind was not armored!

Let's analyze the situation:

- There was no accountability. As soon as Ehud died, the former deliverer, it was sin as usual.
- Captivity came because of rebellion, which resulted in 20 years of harsh bondage.
- Barack interrupted God's standard to set up his own. He lost the honor he would have received. The opportunity was missed because of negligence, which means that someone else would get his honor. Full obedience to God demonstrates honor.

The Fear Factor

- Fear is an unpleasant emotion caused by the belief that something or someone is dangerous and likely to cause pain or threat.
- Fear was Barack's burden. He would rather disobey God than face his fears. He was afraid to rise and go, even though he had a prophetic word. He flatly told Deborah that if she did not accompany him into battle, he would not go.
- Fear is caused by anxious concerns. It is an emotion caused by anxiety or the uneasiness of being afraid of something or someone.

There are various types of fears or phobias that plague the unarmored mind. The psychology of phobias speaks of the adjusting or bending of the normal fear response, regarding a situation or an object that does not present a real danger. The fear is obstructive and intensifies over time as "the fear of fear response." To name a few:

- Astraphobia: The fear of thunder and lightning. Both dogs and people are terrified by this.

- Cynophobia: The fear of dogs, often because of a bad childhood experience.
- Acrophobia: The fear of heights.
- Mysophobia: The fear of germs or dirt.
- Claustrophobia: The fear of being overwhelmed, restricted in a confined space such as an elevator. It can also apply to situations in one's life or relationships. Triggers can include unpleasant experiences, commitment, poverty, or the unknown.[4]

Biochemical Responses to Fear

Epinephrine, also known as adrenaline, is a hormone that is produced by the medulla of the adrenal glands found on top of both kidneys. Powerful emotions such as fear or anger trigger epinephrine to enter the bloodstream, resulting in an increase in heart rate, blood pressure, muscle strength, and sugar absorption. In other words, when adrenaline is released, it signals the brain to redirect energy and blood from the internal organs to the muscles to prepare to fight or flight.[5]

Anger

The Genesis account of two brothers, Cain and Abel, was wise on this. Abel kept flocks, and Cain worked the soil. As time passed, they both brought offerings to God. Cain brought some fruit of the soil, and Abel brought fat portions from the first-born of his flock. Scripture revealed that God looked with favor on Abel's offering, but on Cain's offering, He did not look with favor. Just taking this at face value, it would seem like God was unreasonable, and showing favoritism. However, God shed light on this narrative when He called Cain to task. He asked Cain:

> *Why are you angry? Why is your face downcast? If you do what is right [signifying that there was a right way and a wrong way to bring offerings, and that they both were aware of it], will you not be accepted? But if you do not do what is right, sin is crouching at your door; it desires to have you, but you must rule over it.*[6]

The story revealed later that Cain killed his brother Abel. It was premeditated—he had thought strongly about it, and when the opportunity presented itself, he followed through with it. Evidently, he did not master his thoughts, and so they mastered him. We see here that sinful thoughts crouch at the door to the mind, and desires to dominate. One must desire to master or rule them before they gain entrance and control. Overcoming the battles waged on the battlefields of the mind is paramount. This, however, would require a mind that is fully armored.

Fear and Anxiety

Anxiety in any form can trigger heart attacks, strokes, and other potentially fatal medical emergencies.[7] Too much adrenaline and noradrenaline can be dangerous to the heart, brain, and other organs. Scripture reminds us, in 1 Timothy 1:7, that God has not given us the spirit of fear, but of power, love, and a sound mind.[8] This scriptural relevance explains what the armored mind is all about! Let's face it, according to this inference in Scripture, fear is a spirit, and as a result, it must go! The fear of fear is identified as the spirit of fear. A fearful spirit is self-actualized and very destructive. We are reminded also to be anxious for nothing. Anxiety in a man's heart weighs him down, but a good word makes him glad.[9] The enemy of one's soul uses fear to decrease one's hope and limit one's victories. It is time to release fear and let it go!

How to Break Strongholds Over Your Mind

It is not by might nor by power, but by the spirit of the Lord.[10] Isaiah declared, "The Spirit of the Sovereign Lord is upon me, for He has anointed me.[11] The anointing destroys the yoke of bondage and removes the heavy burden. It causes spiritual adrenaline to be released, bringing about equilibrium in the total being. Things that would have destroyed or weaken you have no more power over you because of the anointing. It is the garment of praise for the spirit of heaviness.[12] To guard the mind against the wiles of the enemy, the mind must be armored. It must not conform to the things of this world but be transformed. The armored mind therefore must:

- Be sober-minded and alert. The adversary, the devil, is like a roaring lion, seeking whom he may devour.[13] One must take control over the thought life of the mind.
- Seek peace and pursue it.[14]
- Study the Word of God.[15]

- Redirect its focus. Meditate or think on things that are good and lovely.[16]
- Be anxious for nothing. Watch and pray daily.[17]
- Listen to the voice of the Holy Spirit.[18]
- Stay in the position where you can make sober decisions.
- Sing songs, hymns, and spiritual songs in worship to God.[19]
- Laugh often. If you can't laugh, take a deep breath and smile.
- Trust in the Lord and wait patiently on Him.[20]

The Apostle Paul, in addressing the Corinthian Church, was led to say:

> *For though we walk in the flesh, we do not war according to the flesh, for the weapons of our warfare are not of the flesh, but divinely powerful for the destruction of fortresses. We are destroying speculations and every lofty thing that raised up against the knowledge of God, and we are taking every thought captive to the obedience of Christ, and we are ready to punish all disobedience, whenever your obedience is complete.[21]*

What Is God Saying to the Armored Mind

Do not allow you mind or your thought processes to put you in bondage. Shun evil and do good. The mind must be girded about with truth. Breakthrough will only come when you know the Truth. For the Truth (Jesus) will make you free![22]

Now that we have shed some light on the importance of having and maintaining an armored mind, the next approach is to do surgery, cutting deep, to expose the internal workings of the mind to apply the remedy.

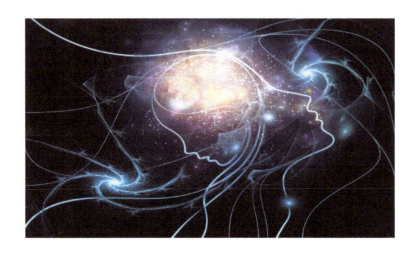

For the Word of God is quick and powerful, and sharper than any two-edged sword, piercing even to the dividing asunder of soul and spirit, and of the joints and marrow, and is a discerner of the thoughts and intents of the heart.

-Hebrews 4:12 KJV

2

THE THOUGHT PROCESSES

Before we begin to make any incision, there are a few things that we must establish. According to Merriam-Webster, thought is defined as "the act of carefully thinking about the details of something." To be more precise, a thought is the result of thinking—a mental attitude. Scripture admonishes us that as a man thinketh in his heart so is he.[23] According to this Scripture, it reveals that a person and their thoughts are one and the same. In the truest sense, you are your thoughts. With this premise, many questions come to mind:

- Can you change or alter your thoughts?
- Can you act outside of your thoughts?
- How do you process your thoughts?
- Who else knows your thoughts?

What Were You Thinking?

This question is often heard when hopes and expectations were not realized. For example, an individual engaged in an assignment that did not meet with satisfaction because of their thought processes. Most of the time, individuals hear what they are listening to, which often is their own thought process. With this approach, how can an employer, a teacher, a mentor, a parent, a spouse or even God get a person to be on the same thought process as themselves? Is it even possible?

Merriam-Webster defines the mind as the element or complex of elements in an individual that feels, perceives, thinks, wills, and especially reasons. The mind chooses the path that it is going to take regardless of instructions. Humans are free moral agents, and as such, exercise their free will based upon their reasoning. They are free from mental micro-management. However, the mentally healthy will give thought to their ways, considering the consequences.

Distractions

An individual can act outside his or her thoughts when it is deemed necessary to do so. This can happen when one is fearful, wants to be accepted, or simply changes one's thought process. For example, a person will align themselves to the dictates of their employer because they need that paycheck. They may go as far as engaging in something against their better judgement because they are fearful, or just want to please. They can become so engrossed in misrepresenting the truth that they start to believe the lie. What used to be an offense to them, has now become the norm. Distractions, because of life's challenges, can also handicap the mindset from functioning at an optimal level, which can greatly hinder productivity. On the other hand, a person who can think outside the box, or who can exercise good judgment, will respond in a positive way, regardless of their view on a matter.

Deception

Self-deception is the worst of deceptions. An individual sometimes reasons within themselves that things are not as bad as they look. This type of self-talk allows their conscious mind to function under false pretense. This creates for them a false security, put together with faulty wiring. As such, they set themselves up for a power failure. Against their better judgement, they succumbed to the power of deception.

Revelation

To stimulate wholesome thinking, it is deemed necessary to do surgery. To get to the internal workings of the mind, you would need a tool that is quick and powerful, and sharper than any double-edged sword. A tool that can cut through the spirit and soul, and through the joints and marrow, and judge the reasoning and conscience of the heart. The Word of God is the only such tool available.

The Word of God is the discerner of the thoughts and intents of the heart. It is the Living Word, a Word with life. A Word that carries the power of life, and the power of transformation. A persistent Word that is active and alive in us until our very spirit and soul, and joints marrow are divided or parted and exposed to God. Jesus, the very Word of God in the flesh, was able to discern the evil thoughts of those who opposed the knowledge of God and set themselves up as weapons of destruction. The people were always taken aback that Jesus not only knew what they were thinking, but the very intent thereof. As a result, Jesus was able to pose questions to them, based on their reasoning.[24]

God sees our thoughts, even before they become knowledge to us.[25] Thoughts are expressed in the heart: When a man's heart is opened, it reveals his thoughts.[26] As a man thinketh in his heart, so is he.[27]

Matthew 15:19 states, "Out of the heart comes evil thoughts." Psalm 94:11 enjoins, "The Lord knows the thoughts of every man." The Word of God cuts down to the bones and marrow because as the Word puts it, "Both the inward thought and the heart of man are deep."[28] As a result, let him who thinks he stands take heed least he falls.[29] Deeds, for the most part, are intimately connected to the decisions of the heart. Most deeds are based on the condition of the heart. God uses the intent of the heart for a true rendition.

Imagination

Imagination is also a process of thinking. There are various disciplines of imagination from a psychological viewpoint, in terms of structure and content. This, however, would be too much of an exhaustive rendition for this presentation. Scripture admonishes us to bring into captivity every thought to the obedience of our Lord, Jesus Christ.[30]

Although imagining and believing are both viewed as cognitive attitudes, they are both vastly different in their motivation. Believing tends to be more proactive. It seeks truth. At the same time, one can be deceived into believing a lie. Eve in the Garden of Eden was deceived by the serpent. She was told by the serpent that if she ate from the forbidden tree, she would not die. As it played out, she did not fall to the ground and die immediately, but gradually. Adam lived nine hundred and thirty years; then he died.[31] The soul that sins shall surely die.[32] It is appointed unto to man once to die and after that the judgment, for the wages of sin is death.[33, 34] By all Scriptural standards, death is inevitable.

By the same token, the imagination can run wild. It has no allegiance or boundaries, and as such, should be harnessed. For example, reins are placed on a horse not to hinder movement, but to maintain control of those movements. Scripture reveals that the Lord searches the heart, and tries the reins, even to give every man according to his ways, and the fruit of his doing.[35] Whoever holds the reins to the mind has the control. The mind, therefore, must be submissive to spiritual counsel and follow clearly defined instructions that will ensure proper functioning. If the horse is not harnessed, it could come near you, creating a hostile environment. If professionally trained, a horse can be engaged in an organized race and emerge victorious. Our minds can be trained when we bring every thought and every imagination to the obedience of Jesus Christ. A Celtic Prayer, "A Scholar's Wish" expressed:

God Help my thoughts! They stray from me, setting off on the wildest journeys ...
They come to me for a fleeting moment, and then away they flee. No chains, no locks can hold them back; no threats of punishment can restrain them ...
They slip from my grasp like tails of eels: they swoop hither and thither like swallows in flight.
Dear, chaste Christ, who can see into every heart and read every mind, take hold of my thoughts. Bring my thoughts back to me and clasp me to yourself.[36]

A scientific experiment conducted on the brain and imagination revealed that, imagining a perceived threat, the brain and the body respond in the same way as experiencing it does. In other words, imagination and reality register the same on the brain. It suggests, "imagination can be a powerful tool in overcoming phobias or post-traumatic stress."[37] However, a sobering thought is how this too can influence the thought processes, which is more reason for imagination to be tempered. David prayed, "Let the words of my mouth and the meditation of my heart be acceptable in Your sight, O Lord, my Strength and my Redeemer."[38]

Be anxious for nothing, but in everything by prayer and supplication, with thanksgiving, let your requests be made known unto God.

-Philippians 4:6

3

THE ANXIOUS MIND

According to the Scripture, anxiety in any form should not be encouraged. Scripture admonishes us to take no thought for our life, what we shall eat, drink, or what we shall put on our body. It goes further to explain that life is more than meat and the body more than raiment.[39] In a society that is often plagued with economic crisis, how is this even possible? Is it even conceivable to believe that a mind can be trained not to be anxious? An anxious mind is not disciplined by prayer and supplication, or with thanksgiving.

Anxiety has been called "the official emotion of our age," the basis of all neuroses, and the "most pervasive psychological phenomenon of our time." It is as old as human existence, but the complexities and pace of modern life have alerted us to its presence and probably increased its influence.[40] The question is, "Why is anxiety a biblical concern?" According to Scripture:

1. It suppresses the very foundation of faith.
2. It undermines the power of God.
3. It confuses the thought processes.
4. It encourages fear and doubt.
5. It can make you sick.
6. It hinders peace.

The Importance of Faith

Faith has everything to do with everything. Without faith, it is impossible to please God. They that come to God must believe that He is, and that He is a rewarder of those who diligently seek Him.[41] The double-minded man is unstable in all his ways, (Ja. 1:8), and therefore, gets nothing from God. When a believer enters prayer, it must be on the grounds of faith. If faith wavers, praying becomes unstable. Faith is such an indelible part of answered prayer, that faith the size of a mustard seed would be answered.[42] Faith in God is processed in the heart of humans. When allowed to function, it greatly affects the anxious mind.

It is not easy to relinquish anxiety, or not to be anxious about anything. People sometimes find it difficult to cast their cares upon the Lord, as He requested.[43] To know when to wait patiently upon the Lord,[44] and when to assume some of the responsibilities in handling a difficult situation, is a matter of prayer. "Anxious people often are impatient people who need help in handling their pressures realistically and within God's perfect time schedule."[45] This would encompass having a personal relationship with the Lord, based on trust.

The Power of God

An anxious mind is not focused on the power of God, but rather has a strong preoccupation with self. Anxiety comes when we turn from God, shift the burdens of life onto ourselves and assume, at least by our attitudes and actions, that we alone are responsible for handling problems instead of acknowledging God's sovereignty and power.[46] Scripture counsels' believers to seek first the kingdom of God and His righteousness.[47] In so doing, all things would be given as well. It must be understood that there is nothing wrong with honestly facing and trying to deal with the identifiable problems of life. To disregard danger is unwise. Our pressing concerns should be committed to God in prayer, who can release us from the grasp of anxiety, to deal realistically with the needs and welfare of life.[48]

Processes in the Mind

The anxious mind pollutes the thought processes through negative thinking. Negative thoughts and meditation foster unwholesome thinking. As a result, the mind becomes confused whether the circumstances are real or imaginary. "Normal anxiety comes to all of us at times, usually when there is some real threat or situational danger. Most often, this anxiety is proportional to the danger (the greater the threat the greater the anxiety). It is anxiety that can be recognized, managed, and reduced, especially when circumstances change. Neurotic anxiety involves intense exaggerated feelings of helplessness and dread even when the danger is mild or nonexistent."[49] When Jesus came walking on the water to his disciples who were in a boat, they cried out, "It is a ghost!"[50] Jesus called out to them, "Take courage, it is I, be not afraid."[51] The word of faith acted as a stabilizer, to direct their minds from a devastated mindset to wholesome thinking.

The Fear Factor

Fear is the anxious mind's worst nightmare. It is the driving force behind anxiety. Anxiety is identified as fear to most writers. It is described as an inner feeling of apprehension, uneasiness, concern, worry, and/or dread that is accompanied by heightened physical arousal. The anxious mind for the most part is propelled by fear. As a result, it stays on constant alert, ready to flee or fight. Scripture admonishes us that God has not given us the spirit of fear, but of power, love, and a sound mind.[52] Having a sound mind positions one to be able to combat the spirit of fear. The spirit of fear hinders progress and stunts productivity. It causes you to have a short attention span, divides your concentration, and so takes away your focus. It also brings about forgetfulness, interferes with problem solving, blocks effective communication, and causes anxiety disorders.

The anxious mind has a strong preoccupation with fear, which hinders performance. A constant replay of past failures or trauma, and an apprehension of making more mistakes or reliving the traumatic experience, is a constant set back. This may include "intrusive disturbing recollections of the trauma, including thoughts, images or perceptions about the incident. The person sometimes experiences recurrent dreams of the incident or feels as though the event was recurring in the present and feels the experience of psychologic distress when internal or external cues resemble the trauma."[53] Such is the case of an individual who experiences post-traumatic stress disorder. Traumatic events can include war, sexual abuse, physical abuse, disasters, accidents, and the grieving process. "Researchers have found that women have almost twice the risk of developing PTSD than do men and that the likelihood increases if the traumatic experience took place before the woman was 15 years old."[54] In addition, there is free-floating anxiety (it has no real external source), and generalized anxiety disorder (excessive anxiety and worries at least six months),[55] all of which are motivated and driven by fear, bringing disturbance to the anxious mind.

Stress

It is a scientific fact that an anxious mind that is bombarded by stress is a recipe for illnesses. "Psychosomatic means mind (psyche) and body (soma). A psychosomatic disorder is a disease which involves both mind and body. Some physical diseases are thought to be particularly prone to being made worse by mental factors such as stress and anxiety."[56] In other words, your mental state can affect how bad a physical disease is at any given time. Some examples are psoriasis, eczema, stomach ulcers, high blood pressure, and heart disease. Medical research has discovered that there are conditions, for example, mitral valve prolapse, a heart abnormality found in 5 to 15% of adults, mostly women, that present no symptoms or need for treatment in over 50% of those affected. The remaining percentage however, experience symptoms associated with panic: chest pain, fatigue, dizziness, shortness of breath, rapid heartbeat, and intense anxiety.[57]

In addition to medication and operations to treat a physical disease, healthcare workers are now focused on the total person, especially when stress related concerns (mental and social factors) are contributing to the disease. Treatment to alleviate stress, depression, or anxiety are incorporated to help slow the effects of the disease. Mental health has become a procurement for physical well-being.

The anxious mind must again consider Philippians 4:6. Be anxious for nothing, but in everything by prayer and supplication and with thanksgiving present your request to God. Based on this counsel, God should not be the person consulted as a last resort but should rather be the first call for help. The downward trend began with a thought. One must capture that thought before it has time to do damage. This is in no way insinuating that a person denies the mental issues that they are experiencing. In fact, admitting fears, insecurities, conflicts, and anxieties when they arise is the initial process of healing. What we want to accentuate is coping mechanisms to help in a time of need. We have already established, from a scientific point of view, that mental processing can inadvertently affect your physical well-being.

Seeking help from God and others in meeting your needs is essential. Praying is very therapeutic, it builds hope, which helps to relax your immune system. Earnest communication with God nourishes your faith, which helps to keep you focused. Thanksgiving takes your mind off your problems. The things of this world go strangely dim in the light of God's glory and grace.[58] Thinking on things that are good and lovely have a way of redirecting your thought processes. Rather than curse the darkness, you can light a light. In so doing, feeding your body the virtues it needs to begin to make amends. If it is true that mental distress worsens your health, then the reverse is true. The mentally healthy will experience abundant life—a byproduct of wholesome living. Healing then starts from within, a position the anxious mind must adapt to or embrace.

Seek Peace

To put it simply, peace is defined as freedom from disturbance, or tranquility. Peace, as it relates to Scripture, includes the notion of totality or completeness, success, fulfillment, wholeness, harmony, security, and well-being. The question is: "How can one have peace in the midst of a world of chaos?" The Bible depicts that in the end times, there will be wars and rumors of wars. Famine, pestilence, and earthquakes would be in diverse places. This is described as the beginnings of birth pains.[59] This surely is not freedom from disturbance, or tranquility. Unfortunately, this provides little hope for inner peace. The question then is: "How can I have peace and maintain it, no matter what the circumstances?" First, you must seek peace and pursue it.[60] Jesus Christ is identified by the Word of God as the Prince of Peace.[61] There is no real peace without Him. Drawing near to God will cause Him to draw near to you.[62] We will look at some of the ways that this can be accomplished. You may not be able to do much about world peace, but you can enjoy Kingdom peace; a recipe for spiritual equilibrium—righteousness, peace, and joy in the Holy Ghost.[63] This is a reassurance to the anxious mind.

You Must Pray for It

Peace responds to prayer. Scripture reminds us not to worry about anything, but in everything, by prayer and supplication with thanksgiving, make your petition know to the Lord.[64] Then the peace of God that passes all understanding will rule you heart and mind through Christ Jesus.[65] It is simple: No prayer, no peace. Believers are urged to pray one for another, that they might be healed.[66] They are obligated to pray for the peace of Jerusalem,[67] also for leaders and governmental authorities, that they may live peaceable lives. Subsequently, wherever you need peace, you must plug into prayer.

Peace Is a Lover of Righteousness

We now know that peace responds to prayer. Peace is also a lover of righteousness.[68] To put this in prospective: When a righteous person prays effectively and fervently, it avails much with God.[69] Love and faithfulness fellowship together, righteousness and peace kiss each other.[70] It is the atmosphere for success, fulfillment, wholeness, harmony, security, and well-being. Great peace is reserved for those who love God's law; as a result, nothing can make them stumble.[71] When God is in control, one can best enjoy inner peace, and consequently, completeness.

The Government of Peace

The peace of God that passes all understanding will rule your heart and mind through Christ Jesus.[72] Peace is identified as a leader, or ruler. When in operation, it will rule and guide the heart and mind to make wholesome decisions. However, the decision makers are the heart and mind, which must be brought into subjection under the leadership of peace. There are two types of peace. Pseudo peace, which calms you for a moment, and the peace of God, that helps you to make sober decisions, no matter what the circumstances are. Jesus exhibited the latter when He was sleeping in a boat in the middle of a storm.[73] The disciples were terrified and cried out to Him for help. Jesus woke up from his rest and rebuked them for having such little faith. Then He commanded the wind and the waves to be still. Suddenly, there was a great calm.[74]

Anxiety is an antagonist of peace. It is hazardous to one's mental health, in that it propels one to make decisions out of convenience, due to fear. As a result, it complicates the situation, rather than resolves it. There are times that you must rise and rebuke the situation, just like Jesus did. He said, "Peace, be still." To rebuke and get the appropriate response, you must take spiritual authority in like manner. This, however, would necessitate a life totally and completely submitted to the will and authority of God. The mind governed by the flesh is death, but the mind governed by the Spirit is life and peace.[75]

Peace Is a Rewarder

Peace rewards a life fully surrendered to the Lord. According to Proverbs 12:20, those who promote peace have joy. This is an immediate remedy for anxiety. The anxious mind finds it difficult to function amidst joy. Scripture declares that the joy of the Lord is your strength.[76] The Apostle Paul encourages believers to sing Psalms, hymns, and spiritual songs, making melodies in their heart.[77] The Bible further attests, "A merry heart does good, like medicine."[78] In contrast, a life consumed by anxiety and distress can lead to medical complications. Romans 14:19 cautions, "Make every effort to do what leads to peace." For this reason, you are blessed when you are a peacemaker. It is a characteristic of the children of God.[79] It stands to reason, then, that our thoughts should be focused on "whatever is true, whatever is noble, whatever is right, whatever is pure, whatever is lovely, whatever is admirable—if anything is excellent or praiseworthy, think about such things. Whatever you have learned or received ... put into practice. And the God of peace be with you."[80] The peace of God will give you peace of mind, equipping you to exercise faith over fear, peace over panic, and God over everything. The virtues of peace are a necessary intervention for the anxious mind.

Say to the captives, 'Come out,' and to those in darkness, 'Be free!'

-Isaiah 49:9 (NIV

4

ISOLATION

Isolation is defined as the state of being alone or away from others. For example, prisoners who are in solitary confinement because of inappropriate behavior. In hospitals, patients are isolated based on their diagnosis.[81] Patients with infectious diseases remain isolated while they are contagious, whether it be strict, respiratory, or protective Isolation. Those in the medical field, while attending to the sick, must wear protective gear so that they do not become infected while treating the disease.[82] So it must be with the teachers and preachers of the Word of God. They must remain unspotted from the things of this world as they minister to the souls of mankind.[83] They must remain under the covering of the blood of Jesus Christ to stay uncontaminated.

Michael E. Carpenter updated five types of isolation in biology.[84] They are:

1. Ecological Isolation. He mentioned that ecological, or habitat isolation, happens when two species that could interbreed are unable to do so because of demographics. The species live in different areas.
   - Spiritually, this type of isolation bears resemblance to those in the body of Christ who are isolated from each other due to social and economic differences.

2. Temporal Isolation. Here he explains that different species who could interbreed do not, because different species breed at different times.
   - In the body of Christ, newborn babes in Christ and mature Christians learn at different paces. Sometimes this keeps them isolated from each other.

3. Behavioral Isolation. This happens, he said, when the population of the same species begin to develop different behaviors that are not identifiable or preferred by members in another population. For instance, many species practice different mating rituals. This could be a song, dance, or a particular scent.

As a result, it would be ignored by the species to which it bears no resemblance.

- Behavioral isolation in relating to the body of Christ reveals that differences in styles of worship can cause isolation in various denominations.

4. Mechanical or Chemical Isolation. This type of isolation takes place because of structures or chemical barriers that keep species isolated from each other. An example is plants not receiving a pollen transfer. Also, certain chemical barriers hinder gametes from forming. Their preference is for sperm from the correct species to fertilize the egg.

- In the body of Christ, there are various denominations, some of which are segregated based on their beliefs and practices. This greatly isolates them from common practices and fellowshipping with each other.

5. Geographical Isolation. This refers to the physical barriers that prevents two species from mating. For instance, a species of monkey that resides on an island cannot mate with another species of monkey on the mainland. The water and the distance between them keep them isolated.

- Spiritual isolation abounds because of sin. It eventually causes one to be eternally separated, or isolated, from God. For this reason, God encourages His children to draw near to Him, and He will likewise draw near to them.[85] Sin is the barrier between humans and God. This hinders fellowship, worship, and ultimately intimacy with God.

Social Isolation

Kelly Burch, in her medical review dated March 26, 2020, about social isolation mentioned how social isolation can negatively affect both mental and physical health. Research findings also attest that social isolation and loneliness are contributors to depression, cognitive decline, poor sleep quality, a weaker immune system, and potential heart problems.[86]

This research was conducted right in the middle of a pandemic. COVID-19 had caused countless families to go into lockdown. Each home was in quarantine, except for essential workers. Many suffered because of this virus—physically, mentally, and emotionally. Loneliness can lead to a 30% increase in the risk of having coronary artery disease and stroke. Researchers are saying, "All our systems, including social, psychological, and biological, have developed around social groups and interaction with one another."[87] For some, this type of isolation had weakened their ability to cope. Suicide threats, as well as mental, verbal, and physical abuse were skyrocketing. It became problematic when the very person or people that one would like to distance from were the same ones that they were lockdown with. This provided extraordinarily little space, in most cases, for distancing. The majority turned to social media for social interaction.

Spiritual Isolation

Say to the captives, "Come out" and to those in darkness, "Be free!"[88] Captivity is recognized as one of the worst types of isolation, whether mentally or physically. The Apostle Paul spoke of his experience that was holding him in bondage from within. This is how he puts it:

> For we know that the law is spiritual,
> but I am carnal, sold under sin.
> For what I am doing, I do not under-
> stand. For what I will to do, that
> I do not practice; but what I hate, that I
> do. If, then I do what I will

not to do, I agree with the law that it is good. But now it is no longer I who do it, but sin that dwells in me. For I know that in me (that is, in my flesh) nothing good dwells; for to will is present with me, but how to perform what is good I do not find. For the good that I will do, I do not do; but the evil I will not do, that I practice. Now if I do what I will not do, it is no longer I who do it, but sin that dwells in me ... I see another law in my members, warring against the law of my mind, and bringing me into captivity to the law of sin which is in my members. O wretched man that I am! Who will deliver me from this body of death? I thank God—through Jesus Christ our Lord![89]

Paul explains that he was a prisoner of the law of sin. We understand that sin is a transgression of God's law, and that the wage of sin is death.[90] The law of sin and death was warring against the law of his mind, bringing him into captivity. He became a slave to sin. Without deliverance, he would be eternally separated from God. Paul also mentioned, in Romans 6:16b, that you are a slave to the one that you obey. Whether you are a slave to sin, which leads to death, or to obedience, which leads to righteousness. "The law was brought in so that the trespass might increase. But where sin increased, grace increased more, so that just as sin reigned in death, so also grace might reign through righteousness to bring eternal life through Jesus Christ our Lord."[91] This remains the only remedy for spiritual isolation.

Reconciliation from Isolation

The Bible declares that humans were on their way to a Christless eternity, alienated from God. Our sins isolate us.[92] Without the shedding of Jesus's blood, there is no pardon for sin.[93] Scripture reminds us that it is by grace that we are saved; it is the gift of God, not by works, lest anyone should boast.[94] It is while we were yet sinners that Christ died.[95] Humans are enemies of God, and not the reverse. God took the initiative—redemption. The gift of God is greater than the trespass. The deceiver (Satan) purposed to alienate people from God. In other words, his role as an accuser is to bring division, through sin of the flesh, to distance humans from God.[96] The prodigal son, after he came to himself from living a life of wantonness, decided to come out of isolation and return home to his father.[97] The father, seeing his son coming from a distance, said, "Quick, bring the best robe, put a ring on his finger and sandals on his feet. Bring the fatted calf and kill it. For this my son was dead and is alive again, was lost and is found."[98] In the same manner, God the Father welcomes every sinner that turns to Him in repentance, through Jesus Christ. Whom the Son sets free, is free indeed.[99] Say to the captives, "Come out," and to those in darkness, "Be free!"[100]

"… their mind is set on earthly things."

-Philippians 3:19

5

MENTAL DISORDERS

As we move further in our exploration of the mind, we will review the thought processes and habits that gives way to mental disorders. What some may describe as mental illness, insanity, or nervous breakdown, professional counselors identify as psychopathology, emotional disturbance, or mental disorder.[101] This delineates a comprehensive variation of symptoms that creates distress or disability in one's personal, social, or occupational life. The symptoms may be mild or severe, to the point where a person may have difficulty co-existing with others and functioning in society becomes problematic. As a result, they may be in persistent danger of self-harm or be an endangerment to others.[102]

Sleep, once referred to as "the gentle tyrant" (Webb, 1992), is one of the human body's biological rhythms, a natural cycle of functioning that the body must experience. There are those biological rhythms that emulates the menstrual cycle of a woman, while others are shorter.[103] "The release of melatonin is influenced by a structure deep within the hypothalamus in an area called the suprachiasmatic [SOO-prah-ki-AS-ma-tik] nucleus, the internal clock that tells people when to wake up and when to fall asleep."[104] Sleep deprivation, or loss of sleep, affects your mental functioning and creates symptoms including trembling hands, inattention, staring off into space, droopy eyelids, and general discomfort.[105]

Depression and manic depression are recognized as mood disorders and affect approximately 10% of the general population. Mood disorders can last throughout one's life span and frequently create personal suffering, problems with relationships, functional impairment, and are a tremendous cost to the healthcare system and society at large.[106] These illnesses often carry a risk of suicide. Major depressive disorder, often referred to as depression, and bipolar disorder, generally known as manic-depressive illness, are two critical mood disorders that constitute severe public health risks that demand immediate attention and long-term treatment.[107] "Depression is the world's leading cause of disease burden or years lost to disability. Bipolar disorder is the seventh cause of disease burden for men and the eighth for women."[108] Mood disorders are identified by subjective mood swings. "Although mood dysregulation is a major sign of these illnesses, other symptoms are also prominent, including changes in physiology, cognition, and behavior."[109] Cardiovascular disease, stroke, cancer, and acquired immune deficiency disorder (AIDS), are also linked to depression, and can affect mobility and mortality.[110]

How a person thinks is intimately connected to how he or she feels. This represents the basic premise of the cognitive views of depression. If our thought processes are negative, this makes depression inevitable. As indicated by psychiatrist Aaron Beck, "depressed people show negative thinking in three areas. First, they view the world and life experiences negatively. Life is a succession of burdens, obstacles, and defeats in a world."[111] Secondly, many depressed people carry a negative image of themselves, which can lead to self-blame and self-pity. Thirdly, they embrace a negative outlook of the future. At times, their thinking is projected in a way to control and influence. Self-condemnation is used manipulatively to gain compliments. For example, saying "I am no good" is a way of getting others to say, "Oh, no, you really are a fine person."[112]

When a person is hurt and if it goes unresolved, they eventually become angry, which hides the hurt. Anger soon progresses to revenge; this hides the hurt and the anger, which results in destructive action or psychosomatic symptoms of depression, which ultimately hides the hurt, anger, and revengefulness.[113] "Some people use depression as a subtle and socially acceptable way both to express anger and to get revenge. The depressed person seems to be saying, 'I'm depressed and miserable, it isn't my fault, and if I don't get attention and sympathy, I may even get more depressed or do something desperate.'" This is viewed as a kind of psychological blackmail.[114] It is often said that hurting people hurt people.

Sin and guilt often lead to depression. When a person sins, they often experience a sense of guilt, because of failure to make the right choices, which often leaves them depressed. The only remedy for sin is repentance and forgiveness. It takes humility to repent. Godly sorrows lead people to repentance.[115] David, when he was experiencing depression, cried out, "Why, my soul, are you downcast? Why so disturbed within? Put your hope in God, for I will yet praise Him, my Savior and my God."[116] David recognized that to escape the place of deep depression, he had to incorporate a right spirit - a spirit of praise. If he kept on rehearsing the hurt, the memory of the insult would continue to haunt him.

Memory is recognized as a process, as well as a place in the brain. It is defined as an "active system that receives information from the senses, puts that information into a usable form, organizes it as it stores it away, and then retrieves the information from storage (adapted from Baddeley, 1996, 2003)."[117] This process is believed to take place through encoding—the set of mental operations that are performed on sensory information to change the information into a configuration that is functional in the brain's storage system.[118] Storage is a place of holding the information for a period of time, and retrieval is the recovering of the material in a form that can be utilized.[119]

Researchers have identified two manifestations of serious memory loss disorders, attributed to complications in the operation of the memory region of the brain. These complications can be results of concussion, brain injury, trauma, alcoholism, Korsakoff's syndrome, or disorders of the aging brain.[120] When an individual receives a head injury because of a vehicle accident, they oftentimes are not able to recall the incident. Sometimes they are incapable of remembering the hours or even days before the accident occurred. They have experienced retrograde amnesia—a loss of memory from the accident backward.[121]

Anterograde amnesia, on the other hand, defines the loss of memory from the point of the injury or illness forward. Alzheimer's patients, at the beginning of the disease, experience anterograde amnesia. At the onset, memory loss may be mild, but then becomes more severe, causing the person to become more forgetful.[122] French professor Bruno Dubois, director of the Institute of Memory and Alzheimer's Disease (IMMA) – Parish Hospitals, in addressing the subject, made this remark, "If anyone is aware of his memory problems, he does not have Alzheimer's'." Those who suffer from a memory illness such as Alzheimer's are not aware of what is happening. As the disease progresses, more dangerous forgetfulness occurs. For example, overmedicating, or cooking food on the stove and leaving it unattended. As the disease progresses, retrograde amnesia takes over, slowly erasing the past.[123] This experience normally brings tremendous stress and grief to the family members and caretakers. They witness the daily deterioration of their loved one, who eventually dies because of the disease.

Grief is viewed as the normal response to loss. Whether it is a significant person, object, or opportunity. Scripture reveals the story of the woman with the lost coin. It mentions that she lost one of her 10 coins. After lighting a lamp and sweeping the floor carefully, she found it. This brought great joy to her heart. She then told her friends and neighbors, and they rejoiced with her.[124] Sad to say, this is not the outcome for everyone who has ever experienced grief. For the most part, there is a sad ending. Most grieving is over the departure of a loved one. For Christians, it is a bittersweet experience. Although they greatly miss their loved ones, they are comforted by the joy of the resurrection.[125]

There are, however, abnormal reactions to grief that are obsessive and complex. This type of grief "is intensified, delayed, prolonged, denied, or otherwise deviating from more normal expressions of sorrow. It is a grief that keeps the mourner in bondage to the deceased person and prevents one from coping and moving on with life."[126] Love (2007) attests those individuals who are experiencing severe functional impairment for more than six months are likely to undergo a complicated grief reaction, and in conjunction may experience comorbid disorders, for instance, anxiety, depression, or PTSD.[127]

Each type of loss endures its own burden. The death of a parent is the most common type of bereavement in adult life. The death of a spouse is more emotional. The burden and stress of living alone and getting on with life can be incredibly stressful. However, the most complicated of all to deal with is the death of a child. Parents often feel guilty, angry, depressed, self-condemning, and incompetent because they failed to protect the child from death (even when there was nothing, they could have done to prevent the death).[128] One study reveals that 70% of grieving parents turn to religion for answers and comfort. The study found that people who turned to God were better able to deal with their losses.[129]

Therefore, having been justified by faith, we have peace with God through our Lord Jesus Christ ... And not only that, but we also glory in tribulations, knowing that tribulation produces perseverance; and perseverance, character; and character, hope. Now hope does not disappoint, because the love of God has been poured out in our hearts by the Holy Spirit who was given to us.

-Romans 5:1-5

6

DIVINE ANTICIPATION

The difference between anxiety and divine antici-pation is hope. Those who experience anxiety are doubtful of their future; therefore, they undergo stress and fear of the unknown. Those who have hope in God have a future.[130] As a result, they experience peace of mind and rest in the knowing; regardless of the circumstances that present them-selves. To anticipate is to expect something to happen. Divine anticipation is to know that it will happen, no matter how long it takes. According to the above-mentioned Scripture, hope does not dis-appoint because of the character that was developed through the process. That process is called persever-ance. Considering this, a person who is perseverant would be on the roadmap to attain their goals. The Apostle Paul attests, "I run ... not with uncertainty.

I fight not as one who beats the air. But I discipline my body and bring it into subjection."[131] This perseverance was only realized because of the trials and hardships that were experienced. The motivator is faith that ensures the peace of God, through Jesus Christ.

Divine anticipation is only possible though the love of God administered through the Holy Spirit. This is the primary reason why hope does not put one to shame. Hope expects, looks, waits, aspires, aims, pants, yearns, longs, hungers, thirsts, and pines. It foresees and foreknows. It is not unfounded optimism, but confident expectation, showing confidence that the end or outcome will be favorable.

Scripture spoke of two individuals who had to wait patiently on God for their miracle. The Bible says about Abraham, in Romans 4:18–21, that against all hope he believed in hope and became the father of many nations. Hope does not deny reality, but it does not depend upon it, either. Without weakening in faith, Abraham faced the fact that his body was as good as dead (he was approaching 100 years old), but he did not waver through unbelief concerning the promise of God (that he would be the father of many nations). He was strong in faith, giving glory to God. He was fully persuaded in his heart that God had the power to perform whatever

He had promised. Abraham kept the faith, and God kept His Word.

There was also a man by the name of Job (Job 1:1–22). The Bible relates a very impressive biography of him. He was regarded as blameless and upright, one who feared God and shunned evil. He had seven sons and three daughters. His possessions included 7,000 sheep, 3,000 camels, 500 yokes of oxen, 500 female donkeys, and a large household. He was regarded as the greatest man in the east.

Now the day came when Job was tested severely. "The Lord said to Satan, 'Have you considered My servant Job, that there is none like him on the earth, a blameless and upright man, one who fears God and shuns evil?'"[132] Satan interjected, "Does Job fear God for nothing? Have you not made a hedge around him, around his household, and around all that he has on every side?"[133] Scripture reminds us that the enemy of humankind watches the righteous and seeks to destroy them. Satan continued, "You have blessed the work of his hands and his possessions have increased in the land. But now, stretch out Your hand and touch all that he has, and he will surely curse You to Your face!"[134] This was a challenge that God was willing to take on because he knew the integrity of Job, his servant. God told

Satan that he could lay his hand on Job, but not take his life.

Unbeknownst to Job, messenger after messenger kept revealing to him his impending doom. Satan orchestrated plans that killed Job's servants by the Sabeans, leaving only one to report the matter. While the servant was still speaking, another servant told him that fire had come from heaven and burned up his sheep and his servants, leaving only one remaining to bear the bad news. While that servant was still speaking, another came and told Job that when his sons and daughters were dining, a strong wind had come and destroyed the house, killing his children in the process. The Scriptures attest that Job got up, tore his robe, and shaved his head. He then fell to the ground and worshipped God. He said, "Naked I came from my mother's womb, and naked I will depart. The Lord gave and the Lord has taken away. May the Name of the Lord be praised."[135] Here again we find praise being offered at a time of great distress. The Bible said that in all that Job went through, he refused to charge God with wrongdoing. Satan was still not satisfied. He asked permission to strike Job's body with a terrible disease. After getting consent, he immediately struck Job's body. It was devastating to the point where worms were eating Job's flesh. Job cried out, "Thou He slay me yet will I serve Him."[136] When his suffering became unbearable, he uttered, "I know that my Redeemer lives, and that in the end I will stand on the earth. And after my skin has been destroyed, I will see Him with my own eyes. I, and not another."[137] This is divine anticipation to the max!

Job's hope in God made him not ashamed. After great trials and testing, Job emerged victorious. God made his later years greater than his former. "… [He] had 14,000 sheep, 6,000 camels, 1,000 yoke of oxen, and 1,000 female donkeys. He also had seven sons and three daughters. Job lived for forty more years and saw his children and grandchildren for four generations."[138] What made Job so confident in hope? According to King David, it is the relationship. "Some trust in chariots and some in horses, but we trust in the Name of the Lord."[139] What is he saying? Although a horse is strong, it cannot save you. In other words, a horse is a vain hope for deliverance.[140] Humankind, for the most part, is oblivious of the spirit world that operates in juxtaposition to their life. Your relationship to God is what gives you the cutting edge. "The horse is made ready for the day of battle—but victory rests with the Lord."[141]

Hope that is deferred, or unduly delayed, can make the heart grow sick.[142] Anxiety disorders are very prevalent during this period of waiting. One could easily become a prisoner of hope in their mind. Things usually happen at just the right time when you are powerless. The Apostle Paul attests, "Be joyful in hope, patient in tribulation.[143] Your struggle is in the waiting. Your waiting must be done in hope. The Lord is our only help and shield.[144] In our struggles, it is imperative that we stay hopeful and exercise faith in every circumstance that we face in life. "Faith is having confidence in what we hope for, and assurance about what we do not see."[145]

Belief is what makes faith possible. The question is: Do you still stand on your convictions, even when you are tested? To believe is not just a mental state; but is demonstrated by action.[146] It is moving from the norm to being radical. Your faith is a tribute to God; it pleases Him. Without faith, it is impossible to please God.[147] One man in Scripture cried out, "Lord I believe, help thou, my unbelief."[148] Faith is a very necessary requirement for answered prayer.

You may have heard the statement "just believe." What does that mean? Webster's definition of believe is to expect with confidence. Let us break this down a little further. To expect means to wait for, to look for something to happen, to anticipate. Confidence denotes a firm belief or trust. Putting this together, we can understand that to believe is to wait, to look for something to happen with a firm belief or trust. In other words, you expect something good is going to happen and you are willing to wait for it, no matter how long it takes. That is faith. It is the substance that we hope for, that which we have not yet seen.[149] It bears repeating. Belief is what make faith possible. If you fail to have confidence, you are going to have speculations, apprehensions, and anxiety. As a result, doubtful thoughts begin to set in, which leads to fear—a trigger for many abnormal behaviors.

Fear is one of the greatest hindrances to success. The "what-ifs" is a struggle. Being unsure of the unknown often leads to instability. Luke 8:3 attests, "Those on the rocky ground are the ones who receive the Word with joy when they hear it, but they have no root. They believe for a while, but in the time of testing, they fall away." When you begin to beat up on yourself for not believing, or put limits on yourself, your answer is to verbalize in prayer, "Lord, I believe, help thou my unbelief."[150] In Luke 8: 40–50, Jairus was told that his daughter was dead, so not to bother the Teacher. Jesus turned to Jairus and said, "Don't be afraid, just believe."

Here is where you must deal with the fear factor or hindrances to your success. The enemy and his cohorts are saying:

- Do not bother to pray.
- Why are you still believing?
- The time has passed.
- You do not have enough.
- It is a dead issue; you cannot do anything about it.
- You are not going to be good enough.
- You are going to fail.

What the enemy is saying is, do not bother the Teacher. The easiest way to lose confidence is when you start listening to those voices, including your own. It is time to put away negative thoughts and just believe. When you take authority over the situation, you will have victory and build confidence. This is achieved when you initiate action by renewing your mind or changing your focus.

Scripture admonishes believers to have the mind of Christ.[151] In so doing, they should no longer be conformed to the things of this world, but be transformed by the renewing of their minds, so that they may attest and approve the will of God.[152] Here the mind can take on the influences of a positive mindset. "A mind dominated by positive emotions becomes a favorable abode for the state of mind known as faith. A mind so dominated may, at will, give the subconscious mind instruction, which it will accept and act upon immediately."[153] True transformation demands positive self-talk that embraces the Word of God. Faith comes by hearing the Word of God.[154] Napoleon Hill affirms that, "Faith is the 'eternal elixir' which gives life, power and action to the impulse of thought."[155] He believes that "faith is the antidote to failure."[156] The responsibility then rests upon the individual to renew their minds to achieve success. To achieve one's definite purpose, will demand a concerted effort on the part of the individual to train their mind to think positively on the Word of God.

The thought processes will assuredly determine the outcome. Napoleon Hill again insists:

> *If you think you are beaten, you are*
> *If you think you dare not, you don't*
> *If you like to win, but you think you can't*
> *It is almost certain you won't*
> *If you think you'll lose, you're lost*
> *For out of the world, we find*
> *Success begins with a person's will—*
> *It's all in the state of mind …*
>
> *Life's battles don't always go*
> *To the stronger or faster man*
> *But sooner or later the one who wins*
> *Is the one who thinks he can!*[157]

Leeford Boohene explains, "Faith is not faith if it is not backed by action. Although Christ commanded the man to stretch out his withered hand (a hand that was drawn in and could not be stretched out), his faith made him to make the effort of stretching out his hand."[158] The logical conclusion is faith needs action. Belief is what makes faith possible. When we doubt, we are questioning God's integrity. Especially, if He has already given you an answer. Sometimes we question the ability of God to do the impossible. God can always perform what He promised, you just need to be fully persuaded that He will.[159]

The question then is: Do we believe, or even trust God? The greatness of God and His proven track record is what we must focus on. Timing has nothing to do with it, seeing that it is impossible for God to lie.[160] Look for whatever you are waiting on to happen, no matter what. You might ask, "How can I stay positive?" Stay in the Word of God. At times, God just wants you to stand still, to see the salvation of the Lord.[161] This is where anything you do might interfere with the process. Listening to God's Holy Spirit will give you direction on how to function in the wait. He will lead and guide you in all truth.[162]

One who has a pure heart and who speaks with grace

will have the King for a friend.

-Proverbs 22:11

7

GRACE BEFORE GREATNESS

Scripture encourages believers to grow in grace and in the knowledge of the Lord Jesus Christ.[163] This type of growth or maturity is highly commended by Scripture, and greatly rewarded. The Bible further reveals that grace and truth came by Jesus Christ.[164] It therefore stands to reason that a follower of Jesus Christ is a follower of grace. To know Him is to know grace.

Jesus's primary reason for coming into the world was to save humankind from their sins. This gift of salvation represents the grace of God. A gift that was not merited or deserving. It is the favor of God, that He sent His only begotten Son to die for the sins of humankind. That those who come to God will not perish but have eternal life (Jn. 3:16). It is while humanity was yet sinners that Jesus died.[165]

The Apostle Paul spoke to the Corinthian church in his letter found in 2 Corinthians 8:1–6 about the grace of God that was bestowed upon the churches of Macedonia. He remarked, "In a great trial of affliction the abundance of their joy and their deep poverty abounded in the riches of their liberality." He explained, "I bear witness that according to their ability, yes, and beyond their ability, they were freely willing, imploring us with much urgency that we would receive the gift and the fellowship of the ministering to the saints. And not only as we had hoped, but they first gave themselves to the Lord, and then to us by the will of God.[166] So, we urged Titus, that as he had begun, so he would also complete this grace in you as well."[167] Paul further counseled, "As much as you abound in everything—in faith, in speech, in knowledge, in all diligence, and in your love for us—see that you abound in this grace also."[168] He told the Corinthians that when you give bread for food, and seed to the sower of God's Word, they would increase their store of seed and the fruit of their righteousness. This results in thanksgiving to God. The recipient of the gift offers great praise to God, and in their prayers, make mention of the giver. The Bible applauds this type of giving as indescribable.[169]

The amazing grace of God can only operate through amazing love. The heart must be an integral part for the hands and feet to operate efficiently. When you are in pain, the body automatically moves to comfort the area that is in distress. Jesus's hands and feet were nailed to the cross, yet His amazing grace flowed down to cover the sins of humankind.

Jesus expects His followers to function in this amazing grace. Walking in grace by any standard is never easy. Grace is best demonstrated in the most severe pain, conflicting trials, and heart-wrenching experiences—places where you are pressed beyond measure. Very few in Scripture have entered this "hall of fame," or better said, "hall of pain." Three such individuals stand out as servants of grace. First, we will look at Queen Esther. There is a story behind Esther's glory. Sometime after Esther had become queen instead of Vashti, Mordecai, her uncle, learned of Haman's plot to destroy the Jews. He sent word to Esther by Hathach to warn her of the plot. The story then commences in (Esther 4:9–17). When Esther heard how her uncle was dressed in sackcloth, she sent garments for him. Mordecai sent back a copy of the written degree of the Jew's destruction to her and requested her to go before the king and plead their cause. Esther was apprehensive at first, fearing for her own life. Anyone who went before the king who was not summoned would be put to death. Mordecai reasoned with her that perhaps she had come to the kingdom for such a time. She, being a Jew, was also included, even though she was queen. Esther's response was to have all the Jews fast and pray for her for three days before she would go in to see the king. In her own words, "If I perish, I perish."[170] God responded, and the amazing grace that Queen Esther demonstrated resulted in her being granted favor by the king.

The Bible spoke about the Apostle Paul in 2 Corinthians 11:22–28, that he was often in prison. He was flogged severely, and often to near death. Five times he received 39 lashes, three times he was beaten with rods, and once he was pelted with stones. He was shipwrecked three times and he spent a night and a day on the open sea. He was constantly on the move. He was in danger from fellow Jews, gentiles, and false believers. He had often gone without sleep and food, naked and cold. In addition, he had the daily pressure of concern for the churches. What kept him going was the amazing grace of God. He was able to say toward the end of his journey in 2 Timothy 4:7, "I have fought a good fight, and I finished my course, I have kept the faith."

The third servant of grace is Jesus Christ. He was no stranger to suffering; Scripture reveals that He was familiar with it.[171] "Who has believed our message and to whom has the arm of the Lord been revealed? He grew up before Him like a tender shoot, and like a root out of dry ground. He had no beauty or majesty to attract us to Him. He was despised and rejected by mankind, a man of suffering and familiar with pain. Like one from whom people hid their faces; He was despised, and we held Him in low esteem. Surely, He took up our pain and bore our suffering; yet we considered Him punished by God, stricken by Him, and afflicted."[172] This great pain that Jesus endured, He could not cast off. He had to drink the bitter cup.[173] You need these contracting pains to push through the passage of life that one must go through. God tempers the race by giving you grace. You can either allow the pain to paralyze you or push through the pain. One politician learned that grace comes before greatness, and failure before fulfillment. History spoke of this individual who:

Failed in business in 1931
Was defeated for the legislature in 1932
Failed in business again in 1934
Lost his sweetheart in 1935

Had a nervous breakdown in 1936
Was defeated in the election in 1938
Was defeated for congress in 1946
Was defeated for congress again in 1948
Was defeated for senator in 1955
Was defeated for vice president in 1956
Was defeated for senate in 1958
Was elected president in 1960 …
His name was Abraham Lincoln.[174]

The question is, what do you do when your pain won't go away? We find in the body of Christ the manifestation of extreme pain, both acute and chronic. The psychological pain that is endured, for the most part, creates distraction and hinders progress, because of the compounded distress. Medication from the Word of God is seldom administered. As a result, healing is poorly managed. God's prescription from His Word remains underutilized, resulting in toxic mindsets. Unbelief and mistrust equal half-empty views, which lack confidence. Unforgiveness and issues of the heart are not remedied due to hurt feelings and wounds. This often develops into fierce anger and bitterness. God wants to heal, restore, and revive His body. God's house is still under construction; His plan is to build a spiritual habitation. The sad thing is that the body has been short-staffed, due to few laborers. The limited supplies have created a spirit of discontentment. The love of many has waxed cold due to unforgiveness—an ongoing distraction. The luster is fading as prayer is at an all-time low, seeing that the lively stones have become sluggish. The Church has been sick. Then, it went on sick leave globally, due to COVID-19. It is time for the Church to report back to duty, not so much the four walls, but kingdom building! It must be healed!

The good news is: The healing is in the pain. The same things that hurt have the potential to heal. It is called the antidote. To administer the serum, you must become the antidote. This is where the grace of God comes in, hence the exhortation to grow in grace and in the knowledge of the Lord Jesus Christ.[175] This is only accomplished when we follow peace with all people,[176] and do what leads to peace.[177] However, this requires complete humility.[178] A shortage of grace leads to bitterness.[179] God's grace is sufficient to the meeting of every need, and purpose is permanent if it is maintained.[180] Only when you let go, and let God have His way will this be achieved.[181]

The heart of an individual can either be broken or become calloused based on your thought processes. David attests that a broken and a contrite heart the Lord will not despise.[182] One is also reminded that the Lord resists the proud but gives grace to the humble.[183] Life is filled with great opportunities, but it is coated in pain. When someone gets burned, they draw back. They resist when it becomes difficult to cope. The Lord is close to the brokenhearted.[184] He heals the brokenhearted and binds up their wounds.[185] If He didn't, spiritual sepsis could set in. At times, God allows the discomfort to continue to develop character. Three times the Apostle Paul asked God to take away the torn in his flesh (a messenger of Satan who buffeted him). The Lord told him that His grace was sufficient, and His strength was made perfect in weakness.[186] When what you are experiencing in life does not make sense, and what you are going through does not equate with your convictions, it becomes your mission—your testimony. What God has placed or allowed in your life—that you see as a hindrance or punishment—represents His grace. He is restraining you for a reason. The King of kings is a friend to the brokenhearted.

Be encouraged; your wounds are not for you. Jesus bore the marks of redemption. His wounds were for you! The pain that He bore brought freedom for humankind. He was wounded for our transgression and bruised for our iniquities. The punishment for our peace was on Him, and by His stripes we are healed[187] – physically, mentally, emotionally, and spiritually. You do not have to hide the emptiness any longer. He heals secret scars. You are called to be stewards of God's grace; use the gift to serve one another.[188] Seeing that you are called by grace, and chosen from your mother's womb,[189] you are responsible to have your conversations be full of grace and seasoned with salt.[190] The choice is always the individual's. To receive grace, one must approach the throne of grace.[191] For it is by grace that you are saved; it is not obtained by works. It is the gift of God, lest anyone should boast.[192]

A joyful spirit is the recipe for endurance. The Apostle Paul declares, "Rejoice in the Lord always. Again, I say, rejoice! Let your gentleness be known to all men. The Lord is at hand."[193] Rejoicing is what keeps our hearts in equilibrium. We are reminded that a merry heart is like medicine,[194] and bitterness is like rottenness to the bones[195]—a great hindrance to joy. It makes a very deep incision in our heart and helps to uproot the root cause that suppresses one's joy. Joel Osteen, in his book *Your Best Life Now* declares, "You must go deeper. You must discover why you are so angry, why you can't get along with other people, why you are always so negative. If you'll look deeply and get to the root, then you'll be able to deal with the problem, overcome it, and truly begin to change."[196] This is deemed very essential for one to continue to experience joy.

Disappointment because of unresolved issues, stifles peace. At times, the wrongdoing may be on your part, which brings on feelings of guilt. "Don't hold on to it and beat yourself up about it. Admit it, seek forgiveness, and move on. Be quick to let go of your mistakes and failures, hurts, pains, and sins."[197] Dr. James Dobson, addressing growth through trial in his book *In the Arms of God* remarked, "The Christian life is a coexistence of both joy and pain."[198] Without this understanding, life becomes a burden. Sometimes an individual may be angry with God for not coming through for them as they wanted him to. Dr. Dobson added, when this happens, "there is only one cure for the cancer of bitterness: To forgive the perceived offender, once and for all, with God's help."[199] The Bible states that, "If we confess our sins, He is faithful and just to forgive us our sins and purify us from all unrighteousness."[200] When this takes place, a person is free to rejoice!

Researchers have found that "just looking forward to a positive and humorous laughing experience can significantly decrease levels of potentially damaging hormones: cortisol, a major stress hormone, epinephrine (adrenaline), and DOPAC, a brain chemical that helps produce epinephrine."[201]

In other research, they discovered that "repetitive, joyous laughter causes the body to respond as if receiving moderate exercise, which enhances mood and immune system activity, lowers both bad cholesterol and blood pressure, raises good cholesterol, and decreases stress hormones".[202] In everything give God thanks; this is His will concerning you.[203] It is a natural antidote for healing. God is concerned with the health of the total person. The benefits far outweigh the hardships. Those who listen to the Holy Spirt represent the true children of God.[204] Human weakness provides the ideal opportunity for the display of divine power. God's power is made perfect in weakness.

I will praise You because I have been remarkably and wondrously made. Your works are wondrous, and I know this very well.

-Psalm 139:14 (CSB)

8

GREAT MINDS

It is often stated that great minds think alike. Greatness is not hereditary, but rather cultivated. Most of the time greatness in its embryo stage is exceedingly small. Scripture reminds us that God uses weak things to confound the wise.[205] The disciples of Jesus Christ, in particular Peter, were viewed as ignorant and unlearned men, yet they are responsible for the growth and spread of Christianity as we know it today. After the first sermon that Peter preached, thousands came to know Jesus as their personal Lord and Savior.[206] They were not daunted by the hardships that they suffered. Moreover, the Apostle Paul was led to say, "If we are children, then we are heirs—heirs of God and co-heirs with Christ, if indeed we share in His sufferings in order that we may also share in His glory."[207] They rejoiced that they were counted worthy to suffer shame for His name.[208] As a result, with singleness of purpose, they were most determined to spread the Gospel without regard to fear or fame. Their love for Jesus Christ constrained them from any such indulgence.[209] Following are the biographies of some individuals who otherwise are viewed as minorities, who took on the initiative to push themselves in what they believed and emerged victorious. They simply defied the thought processes of the masses and proceeded to focus on their own mindsets to be the best that they could be. As a result, they most likely exceeded their own expectations.

Dr. Daniel Hale Williams, born in 1856, was the first surgeon to successfully perform an open-heart surgery in the United States. Williams also founded the first interracial hospital in the country. He was born in Pennsylvania in 1856, to Sarah Price Williams and Daniel Hale. After an unrewarding effort as a barber and a shoemaker, he decided to further his education. He started out as an apprentice to Dr. Henry Palmer, then continued his medical training at Chicago Medical College.[210]

African Americans were prevented from being admitted to hospitals, and black doctors were refused the hiring process. Williams felt it was important to have interracial hospitals, where black and white doctors could learn together. As a result, in May 1891, Williams successfully opened the Provident Hospital and Training School for Nurses, the first interracial hospital and nursing school in the country.[211]

His pioneering surgery occurred in the summer of 1893. James Cornish, who had been stabbed in the chest, was brought to Provident Hospital, according to the Provident Foundation, which helps fund the hospital and preserve its legacy.[212] The procedure was done without the modern amenities of X-rays, antibiotics, surgical prep-work, and other modern equipment. Cornish walked out of the hospital 51 days later.

Williams soon became the head surgeon at the most prestigious hospital for black patients, Freedman's Hospital in Washington, DC. In 1902, he performed another pioneering surgery on a damaged spleen. Williams continued to practice medicine well into his 70s, until he suffered a stroke in 1926. He then retired, until his death in 1931, according to the Provident Foundation.

Christine Darden, born in 1942 in North Carolina, was a skilled mathematician, data analyst, and aeronautical engineer.[213] After working at NASA for over 40 years, she became one of the world's experts on sonic boom prediction, sonic boom minimization, and supersonic wing design, according to NASA.[214] She earned a bachelor's degree in mathematics as well as a teaching certificate before working as a teacher in Portsmouth, Virginia, and at Virginia State College.

In 1967, Darden, whose life was also chronicled in the book *Hidden Figures*, became a "human computer" for NASA's Langley Research Center (Darden was not depicted in the movie *Hidden Figures*.) After eight years, she approached her supervisor and asked why men with the same level of education as she had been hired as engineers while she wasn't. Shortly after, she was transferred to the engineering section, where her first assignment was to write a computer program for sonic boom.

She spent the next 25 years working on sonic boom minimization. In 1983, she earned a doctorate degree in mechanical engineering at George Washington University, and in 1989 she became the technical leader of NASA's Sonic Boom Group of the Vehicle Integration Branch of the High-Speed Research Program. In 1999, she became the director of the Program Management Office of the Aerospace Performing Center. Throughout her career, she also served as a technical consultant on government and private projects and authored more than 50 papers in high-lift wing design.

Now she encourages people, including her children, her grandchildren, and her great-grandchildren to always be curious. "I was able to stand on the shoulders of those women who came before me, and women who came after me were able to stand on mine," Darden said, according to NASA.[215]

Emmett Chappelle, born in 1925, was an American biochemist who made groundbreaking discoveries in the understanding and application of bioluminescence, or the ability of living organisms to produce light.

Chappelle was born in Phoenix, and after graduation from high school, he was drafted into the army during World War II. When he returned to the United States, he earned an associate's degree in electrical engineering from Phoenix College, and then enrolled at the University of California, Berkeley, where he graduated with a degree in biology in 1950, according to Woods Hole Oceanographic Institution.[216] Chappelle went on to earn a master's degree at the University of Washington, and started a PhD at Stanford University.

After he left Stanford, he was offered a position at the Research Institute for Advanced Studies in Maryland, where he studied ways to ensure breathable air for astronauts. In 1963, Chappelle began work at Hazleton Laboratories in Virginia, which held contracts with NASA. There, he studied ways to detect extraterrestrial life on planets such as Mars. It was there that Chappelle invented a revolutionary scientific test known as the ATP fluorescent assay, which detects living cells by making them glow.[217]

His test would go on to have widespread applications in agriculture and medicine. Chappelle was awarded NASA's Exceptional Scientific Achievement Medal in 1994. His life's work contributed to the growth and development of technology, offering mentorship to minority high school and college students.[218]

Gladys West, born in 1930, was key in developing the GPS technology that allows satellites to locate you anywhere on Earth—and yet, she herself remained a "hidden figure" for more than five decades.

West was born Gladys Mae Brown in Sutherland, Virginia, part of a rural county south of Richmond. Not eager to work in the tobacco fields or factories where her family worked, West devoted herself to her education. When she graduated as valedictorian from her high school, she won a full scholarship to Virginia State College, where she earned both a bachelor's and a master's degree in mathematics by 1955.[219]

When she began working at a military base in Dahlgren, Virginia, known as the Naval Proving Ground (now called the Naval Surface Warfare Center), West was the second black female ever hired there and one of just four black employees. She started as a human computer, solving complex equations longhand, before becoming a programmer on some of the earliest supercomputers. In the 1960s, West participated in award-winning research that proved the regularity of Pluto's orbit relative to Neptune (for every two orbits that Pluto makes around the sun, Neptune makes three). Beginning in the 1970s, she programmed an IBM computer to precisely model the irregular shape of Earth (also known as the geoid).[220] The data generated by West's complex algorithms ultimately became the basis for the Global Positioning System (GPS). West's contribution to that now-ubiquitous technology went largely unrecognized until she casually mentioned it in a speech to her former sorority, Alpha Kappa Alpha. Following an Associated Press profile of her in 2018,[221] the U.S. Air Force published a press release finally paying tribute to her accomplishments.[222]

James West, born in 1931, is an inventor, former Bell Laboratories engineer, and physicist at John Hopkins University.

West's most famous invention is the foil electret microphone, now the most commonly used microphone in the world, according to Johns Hopkins University (JHU).[223] The device, which West designed with collaborator Gerhard Sessler, was originally designed for a team of acoustical psychologists who needed small and sensitive instruments to study human hearing, according to the African American History Program (AAHP)[224] of the National Academies of Science, Medicine, and Engineering. The compact, inexpensive device West and Sessler designed is now used in applications ranging from cell phones to hearing aids to professional music equipment.

West has continued to research microphones and other acoustic technologies "for air and water" applications, according to JHU, and has also written numerous books and papers on solid-state physics and materials science. Capping his many professional honors, West was awarded the National Medal of Technology, the United States' "highest award for technological innovation."

Benjamin Banneker, born in 1731, was a mathematician, astronomer, farmer, and surveyor who was born in England's American colonies and lived through the early years of the United States.

Banneker's father was a former slave who his mother, the daughter of a former slave and an English colonist—had purchased, freed, and married, according to a biography by Scott Williams, a mathematician at the University of Buffalo.[225] Despite lacking a formal education in the subjects, Banneker became known for his skill in mathematics and astronomy.

He "successfully predicted the solar eclipse that occurred on April 14, 1789, contradicting the forecasts of prominent mathematicians and astronomers of the day," Williams wrote. In 1791, President George Washington appointed Banneker to a three-man team assigned to survey the site that would become Washington DC. In that same period, he began work on his most famous project: *Banneker's Almanac.* [226] The six volumes, published between 1792 and 1797, included information about astronomy, medicine, and future eclipses, as well as subjects such as astrology that are no longer considered scientific.[227] Banneker wrote a 12-page letter to Thomas Jefferson in 1971, the secretary of state and future president who advocated white supremacy, and argued that black people were not inferior. Enclosing his first almanac, he attacked Jefferson's "absurd and false ideas." It is said that in the letter, "Banneker then respectfully chided

Jefferson and their patriots for their hypocrisy, enslaving people like him while fighting the British for their own independence."[228]

Jesus Christ is arguably the greatest person ever to have lived. He is esteemed as the epitome of greatness. Scripture attests, being found in the form of man, He humbled Himself, and became obedient to death, even death on a cross.[229] The Bible refers to Jesus as the King of the Jews, yet He had a humble beginning in a stable, where He was born.[230] Very few were alerted of His birth, yet today, billions have applauded His life. His purpose— the salvation of humankind—is undeniable to His followers, who glorify Him as Lord. The passion and ultimate death of Jesus Christ is the foremost display of an incredible love for humanity.[231] Jesus declared that He did not come to be served, but to serve and give His life a ransom for many.[232] Humility is foremost one of His prized traits. He was led as a lamb to the slaughter, yet he opened not His mouth. Even though He was lied upon, mocked, jeered, spat upon, flogged, insulted, blasphemed, and endured all manner of abuse to the point where His visage was marred.[233] "He bore our sins in His own body … that we, having died to sin, might live for righteousness—by whose stripes you were healed."[234] The Bible declares that God so loved the world that

He gave His only begotten Son that whosoever believes in Him would not perish, but have everlasting life.[235] God did not send His Son to condemn the world, but that the world through Him might be saved.[236] Incredible, while Jesus was on the cross, amidst insults, He asked his Father to forgive the people. In His own words, "They know not what they do."[237]

Jesus stood the test and remained victorious over death.[238] The eternal life of humanity rested on Him. Considering Himself was out of the question. It was all about fulfilling the will of His Father, regardless of personal repercussion. Jesus had a made-up mind to fulfill the desires of His Father. As a result, He was commended for it.[239] Jesus went about doing good, including healing the sick.[240] Jesus is looked upon as the Great Physician and the Church a hospital.[241] Jesus declared, "I will build my Church and the gates of hell will not prevail against it."[242] This assurance brings hope to the hurting, whether the pain is physical, emotional, or spiritual. He specializes in mending the brokenhearted and setting the captives free. He is touched by the feeling of our infirmities, and as a result He is compassionate to us all.[243]

Personal Testimony

I came to know Jesus Christ as my personal Lord and Savior at a young age. From my early recollection of Him, He has always shown me grace and mercy. His love is very personal—tailor-made to my needs. My most choice possession is the relationship that we share. He gives me heart support and counsel. I remember after I had failed my NCLEX examination, I was distraught, to the extent where I was close to depression. Then the Lord said to me, "I am the Great Physician, and you have the training. We have a hospital to run!" Being a pastor, I knew exactly what He meant. That was the most rewarding and beneficial thing that He could have said to me at the time. I was quickened in my spirit to rise and begin to pursue His purpose with understanding. You see, my mind was set on working in the medical field. It was a passion for me, and I was preparing myself to seek employment. God's plan in the process was for me to understand my employment. God is the creator of humankind; He is the maker of the very discipline that I was studying, anatomy and physiology, and dealing with the various diseases and abnormalities that affect that structure. As a result of this divine intervention, my approach to this discipline was revolutionized. Having a better understanding of this process, coupled with spiritual implications ... well, this book is a direct result of that reconciliation! Having the mind of Christ is imperative and very essential in a life plagued with hardships and pain. It is the very platform upon which the thought process and the anxious mind must abide.

The Spirit of God is the Holy Spirit. Jesus affirms that the Holy Spirit is a Comforter, who will lead and guide believers into all truths, because He goes to the Father.[244] He functions in you and with you, who are born again by the Spirit of the Lord. He represents the Wisdom of God, who will help you with all decision-making. As we remain open before the Lord, He can pour into us any remedy that our soul and spirit may need, upon request. Jesus remains the Author and Finisher of our faith.[245] He desires for us to have endurance in the race that is before us.[246] Also, to run that we would obtain the prize of the high calling in Him.[247] An armored mind has its rewards. It is always grace before greatness. In this way, we maintain spiritual and emotional health, and we are not eternally isolated from Him. This divine anticipation is the beginning of having a great mind that is mentally and spiritually sound. "I will praise You because I have been remarkably and wondrously made. Your works are wondrous, and I know this very well."[248]

Looking back
God has been faithful

APPENDIX A

SELF-EXAMINATION

- **THE THOUGHT PROCESSES— WHAT ARE YOUR AREAS OF CONCERN AND WHY?**
    - o DISTRACTION...................................
      ....
      ....
    - o DECEPTION...................................
      ....
      ....
    - o IMAGINATION...................................
      ....
      ....

- **THE ANXIOUS MIND**
    - o HOW IMPORTANT IS FAITH IN YOUR RELATIONSHIP WITH GOD?
      ....
      ....
      ....

    o THINGS THAT YOU ARE FEARFUL OF AND WHY?

        ....

        ....

        ....

    o STRESSORS IN YOUR LIFE

        ....

        ....

        ....

- **ISOLATION**
  - o DO YOU FEEL REJECTED? WHY?

        ....

        ....

        ....

- **MENTAL DISORDER**
  - o WHAT THINGS HAVE CAUSED YOU TO FEEL DEPRESSED? WHY?

        ....

        ....

        ....

- **DIVINE ANTICIPATION**
  - o WHAT ARE THE AREAS IN YOUR LIFE WITH WHICH YOU HAVE TRUST ISSUES?

    ....

    ....

    ....

- **GRACE BEFORE GREATNESS**
  - o WHAT HAS CAUSED YOU GREAT PAIN OR BITTERNESS?

    ....

    ....

    ....

- **GREAT MINDS**
  - o DO YOU FEEL INSIGNIFICANT OR INFERIOR? WHY?

    ....

    ....

    ....

APPENDIX B

MY PRAYER

D ear God, first I want to thank You for allowing this book to be published. I pray that every person who reads this book will experience supernatural empowerment and enrichment from the Holy Spirit. Whether this person is a schoolteacher, a corporate executive, a factory worker, a mom, a dad, a child, a believer, or an unbeliever. I pray that clarity will be imparted, and that it will bring forth a greater handling of the circumstances that come their way, and their relationship with people in general. I pray that they will be able to sit in the driver's seat and make informed decisions that would create harmonious relationships and ultimately, a more peaceful environment. I pray that the information in this book will help them in directing and channeling their thoughts to be more productive in their life's pursuits. Revolutionize the life of every reader, dear God, and that they will seek to use the information herein to benefit themselves and others. Through study groups, workshops, church growth, and leadership training. I pray for the supernatural success of this book! That it will motive people to good works! As a result, that it will inspire change. I pray that this transformation will impact the hearts of individuals in their homes, marriages, family relationships, work relationships, and most importantly, their relationship with You, God. I also pray for the financial success of this book. This I ask, in Jesus' precious name. Amen.

WHAT IS YOUR PRAYER?

....
....
....
....
....
....
....
....
....
....
....
....
....
....
....
....
....
....
....
....
....
....
....
....

ABOUT THE AUTHOR

APOSTLE DR. SANDRA MITCHELL

Reverend Sandra Mitchell is an accomplished woman of God. She has over 25 years' experience as a strategic planning director with focus on development and growth. Over the years, she has developed strong interpersonal skills in her line of duty. God has gifted Rev. Mitchell with competence in counseling with conflict resolution strategies. She also writes and develops policy procedures with emphasis on compliance. Rev. Mitchell is also the project manager for Daystar Steel Band, an evangelistic tool used in outreach ministry. Through this evangelistic arm, God has used her to minister in various cities across the United States, through music, preaching, and prophesying. Many souls have been saved and delivered. Other opportunities for ministry have taken her to Panama, the Republic of Haiti, Antigua, St. Vincent, and the Grenadines.

God uniquely positioned Rev. Mitchell as the Co-founder and CEO of Daystar Ministries of Fort Lauderdale Inc. Dba Daystar Connect, and Founder and CEO of Freedom Reigns Global Restoration Convention. She is an ordained Apostle, Prophetess and Senior Pastor of said ministry.

Prophetess Mitchell has an incredible anointing for women. She is the founder and president of Women of Wisdom (W.O.W.), Adopt a Child Program (A.A.C.P.), Adopt a Family Program (A.A.F.P.), and Mothers on Morals International (M.O.M.I.). She also founded and headed the Fort Lauderdale branch of Women with a Call International for 14 years.

Apostle Mitchell is an accomplished workshop coordinator and facilitator, who God is using to provoke the body of Christ to good works. She holds an Associate of Science Degree in Nursing from Lincoln College of Technology, a Bachelor of Ministry Degree (magna cum laude), and a Master of Theology Degree from International Seminary, Plymouth, Florida. She also has attained an honorary degree, a Doctor of Divinity from Community

Bible Institute & Seminary Brevard, Inc. One of her ambitions is to propagate the Gospel through medical evangelism, and the publication of books. Dr. Sandra Mitchell wants it to be known that she loves the Lord with all her heart. She surrendered her life to Him at an early age, and ever since has strived to get closer and closer to Him. Her passion is for Christ, and as a result, she cherishes her position as the bride of Christ.

Apostle Dr. Sandra Mitchell is the widow of the late Apostle Dr. Ernest Mitchell, founder of Daystar Ministries of Ft. Lauderdale Inc. She is called to do apostolic work through the Discipleship of Nations. She is gifted in mentorship—the training and development of leaders. She is a true worshipper with a global mandate to promote righteousness to the nations through the delivery of the Word of God, including the writing and publication of books.

THE ARMORED MIND

BREAKING STRONGHOLDS OVER THE MIND

In this anointed book, Apostle Dr. Sandra Mitchell effectively tackles a complex subject and substantively contributes to the ongoing quest to further our understanding of the workings of the human mind.

-Derek H. Suite, M.D., M.S.
Founder & CEO Full Circle Health, PLLC
www.fullcirclehealthny.com

A deep wellspring of spiritual waters—this is how I would define Apostle Dr. Sandra Mitchell. "And men of understanding will draw from it," is the proverbial wisdom for those seeking to find such a well in their lifetime. Apostle Mitchell has been a source of spiritual nurturing for many desiring deeper growth and transformation within. I, myself, am a beneficiary and have learned to embrace my life's purpose and God-given identity with her guidance supporting me.

-Dr. Therese McFarlane
clinical consultant, pastor & prophetess at
The Healing Place Global Church,
and author of *Awake Anew: Living the True You*

Dr. Sandra Mitchell has a remarkable heart for people with an eye for seeking out opportunities to make an impact in the community. I have found Dr. Mitchell to be a natural leader who stands strong in her beliefs and strives to get the best results. Dr. Mitchell brings a unique energy, optimism, passion, and tireless creativity to all her endeavors.

-Dr. Sherron Parrish, Ph.D.
founder & CEO of Fountain of Life Ministries

Unwavering commitment and complete devotion to Almighty God, impressing and inspiring, Apostle Dr. Sandra Mitchell exudes humility, dignity, and grace. Dr. Mitchell, a true lover of humanity, is a prolific conference organizer, a dynamic conference speaker, life coach, Teacher, preacher, counselor, and medical professional. Dr. Mitchell's book, *The Armored Mind*, is an embodiment of her expertise, a powerhouse of Biblical philosophies, relevance, and applications. It is compelling and riveting, an absolute must read; it delivers without compromise!

-Reverend M. Grace Kelly

author, chaplain, auditor,
certified financial counselor

Dr. Sandra Mitchell, apostle, leader, prophetess, teacher, and author has a profound gift of engaging her audience so that they comprehend the depth of the message and apply it to their lives.

-Dr. Debra A. Allen

apostle, specialist in community college teaching,
doctor of Christian education

If anyone is qualified to speak on *The Armored Mind – Breaking strongholds over the Mind*, is Dr. Sandra Mitchell. I've witnessed this woman of God overcome so many attacks of the enemy. This book will show you how to develop an armored mindset that strongholds over your mind will be broken and destroyed. Then you can be successful in life.

-Overseer Apostle Priscella McCoy

Author – When Hurt Doesn't Hurt Anymore
Rivers of Life Restoration Ministries,
New Port Richey, Fl.

Apostle Dr. Sandra Mitchell provides practical and sensible solutions in her book, *The Armored Mind – Breaking Strongholds Over the Mind*. Something that is needed in the Body of Christ today. This book is simple refreshing, a usable guide that will help you in your Spiritual journey.

-Apostle Dr. Oswald T. Felix
El Shaddai Bible Ministries Inc.

ENDNOTES

The scriptures used in this book are taken from the Holy Bible, the New King James Version, unless otherwise stated.

Chapter 1: Breaking Strongholds of the Mind

Apostle Dr. Sandra Mitchell

CEO and President Daystar Ministries
of Ft. Lauderdale, Inc.
DBA Daystar Connect
website: DrSandraMitchell.com
Email: sandraamitchell@gmail.com
Phn. (954) 601-6105

1   Judges 4:1.

2   Judges 4:3.

3   Judges 4:9.

4   A 1998 Survey of more than 8,000 respondents published in the British Journal of Psychiatry, *https://www.nicolehuthwaitetherapy.co.uk.*

5   Fritscher, Lisa. "What is Fear?" *Verywellmind*, medically reviewed by Daniel B. Block Md. On June 19, 2020, https://www.verywellmind.com.

6   Genesis 4:6–11.

7   Cherney, Kristeen. "12 Effects of Anxiety on the Body." *Healthline*, medically reviewed by Timothy J. Legg, PhD., updated August 25, 2020, https://www.healthline.com.

8   1 Timothy 1:7.

9   Proverbs 12:25.

10   Zechariah 4:6.

11   Isaiah 61:1.

12   Isaiah 61:3.

13   1 Peter 5:8–9.

14   1 Peter 3:11.

15   2 Timothy 2:15.

16   Philippians 4:8.

17   Matthew 26:41.

18   John 16:13.

19   Ephesians 5:19.

20   Proverbs 37:7.

21   2 Corinthians 10:3–6.

22   John 8:32.

Chapter 2: The Thought Processes

23   Proverbs 23:7.

24   Luke 7:39–42.

25   Psalms 139:1–2.

26   Psalms 26:2.

27   Proverbs 23:7, KJV.

28   Psalms 64:6.

29   1 Corinthians 10:12.

30   2 Corinthians 10:5, KJV.

31   Genesis 5:5.

32   Ezekiel 18:20.

33   Hebrews 9:27.

34   Romans 6:23.

35   Jeremiah 17:10.

36   Dallman, Christine A. and Margaret Anne Huffman. *My Personal Daily Prayer Book*. Publications International, 2009.

37   Scientific experiment conducted by the University of Colorado at Boulder on the subject: *Your Brain on Imagination*, Neuroscience News.com.

38   Psalms 19:14.

Chapter 3: The Anxious Mind

39   Matthew 6:25.

40   Collins, Gary R. *Christian Counseling: A Comprehensive Guide.* Revised edition, Word Publishing, 1988, 78.

41   Hebrews 11:6.

42   Matthew 17:20.

43   1 Peter 5:7.

44   Psalms 27:14.

45   *Christian Counseling*, 79–80.

46   Ibid, 79.

47   Matthew 6:33.

48   *Christian Counseling*, 79.

49   Ibid.

50   Matthew 14:26.

51   Matthew 14:27.

52   2 Timothy 1:7.

53   Fortinash, Katherine M. and Patricia A. Holoday Worrett. "The Brain on Imagination." *Psychiatric Mental Health Nursing*, fifth edition, Elsevier Mosby, 2012, 193.

54   Ciccarelli, Saundra K. and J. Noland White. *Psychology.* Third edition, Prentice Hall, 544.

55   Ibid.

56   "Psychosomatic Disorders or Mind-Body Disorders." *Neurosciences*. hoag.org/specialties-services/neurosciences/contact-us/.

57   *Christian Counseling*, 83.

58   Jackson, Alan, singer. April 3, 2008.

59   Matthew 24:7–8.

60   Psalms 34:14.

61   Isaiah 9:6.

62   James 4:8.

63   Romans 14:7.

64   Philippians 4:6.

65   Philippians 4:7.

66   James 5:16.

67   Psalms 122:6.

68   1 Timothy 2:2.

69   James 5:16.

70   Psalms 85:10.

71   Psalms 119:165.

72   Philippians 4:6.

73   Matthew 4:24–25.

74   Matthew 4:26.

75   Romans 8:6.

76   Nehemiah 8:10.

77   Ephesians 5:19.

78   Proverbs 17:22.

79   Matthew 5:9.

80   Romans 4:8–9.

Chapter 4: Isolation

81   *Your Dictionary.* "Isolation." yourdictionary.com/
isolation.

82   "Guidelines for Isolation Precaution in Hospitals," *CDC Wonder.* wonder.cdc.gov>wonder>prevguid.

83   James 1:27.

84   Carpenter, Michael E. "5 Types of Isolation
in Biology," updated May 09, 2018.
sciencing.com/five-types-isolation.

85   James 4:8.

86   This article was medically reviewed by Mayra Men-
dez, Ph.D., LMFT, a licensed psychotherapist at Provi-
dence Saint John's Child and Family Development Center.
static/insider.com/
how-social-isolation.

87   Ibid.

88   Isaiah 49:9.

89   Romans 7:14–25.

90   Romans 6:23.

91   Romans 5:19–21.

92   Colossians 1:21.

93   Hebrews 9:22.

94   Ephesians 2:8–9.

95   Romans 5:8.

96   Revelation 12:10.

97   Luke 15:13–19.

98   Luke 15:22–24.

99   John 8:36.

100   Isaiah 49:9.

Chapter 5: Mental Disorders

101   Collins, Gary R. Christian Counseling: *A Comprehensive Guide*. Revised edition, Word Publishing, 1988, 470.

102   Ibid.

103   Ciccarelli, Saundra K. and J. Noland White. *Psychology*. Third edition, Prentice Hall, 131.

104   Ibid, 132.

105   The Effects of Sleep Deprivation on your body, https://www.healthline.com >

106   Fortinash, Katherine M. and Patricia A. Holoday Worrett. "The Brain on Imagination." *Psychiatric Mental Health Nursing*, fifth edition, Elsevier Mosby, 2012, 218.

107   Ibid.

108   Ibid.

109   Ibid.

110   Ibid, 219.

111   *Christian Counseling*, 108.

112   Ibid.

113   Ibid, 109.

114   Ibid.

115   2 Corinthians 7:10.

116   Psalms 43:5.

117   *Psychology*, 214.

118   Ibid.

119   Ibid, 214, 215.

120   Ibid, 243.

121   Ibid.

122   Ibid, 244.

123   Ibid.

124   Luke 15:8–10.

125   John 11 :25–26.

126   *Christian Counseling*, 347.

127   *Psychology*, 646.

128   *Christian Counseling*, 348.

129   Ibid.

Chapter 6: Divine Anticipation

130   Jeremiah 29:11.

131   1 Corinthians 9:26–27.

132   Job 1:8.

133   Job 1:10.

134   Job 1:10–11.

135   Job 1:21.

136   Job 13:15.

137   Job 19:25–27.

138   Job 42:12–16.

139   Psalms 20:7.

140   Psalms 33:17–20.

141   Proverbs 21:31.

142   Proverbs 13:12.

143   Romans 12:12.

144   Psalms 33:20.

145   Hebrews 11:1.

146   James 2:26.

147   Hebrews 11:6.

148   Mark 9:24.

149   Hebrews 11:1.

150   Luke 8:40–50.

151   1 Corinthians 2:16.

152   Romans 12:2.

153   Hill, Napoleon. *Think and Grow Rich*. Revised and expanded by Dr. Arthur R. Pell, Jeremy P. Tarcher/Penguin, 2005, 48.

154   Hebrews 6:18.

155   *Think and Grow Rich*, 49.

156   Ibid.

157   Ibid, 55.

158   Boohene, Leeford. *Stretch your Faith: How To Experience The Supernatural*. Arthur & Associates, 2015, 63.

159   Romans 4:21.

160   Hebrews 6:18.

161   Exodus 14:13.

162   John 16:13.

Chapter 7: Grace before Greatness

163   1 Peter 3:18.

164   John 1:17.

165   Romans 5:8.

166   2 Corinthians 8:3–5.

167   2 Corinthians 8:6.

168   2 Corinthians 8:7.

169   2 Corinthians 9:6–15.

170   Esther 4:16.

171   Isaiah 53:3.

172   Isaiah 53:1–4.

173   Matthew 26:39.

174   Me.me/i/are-you-easily-discouraged-failed-in-business-31-defeated-for-22068431.

175   2 Peter 3:18.

176   Hebrews 12:14.

177   Romans 14:19.

178   James 4:6.

179   Hebrews 12:15.

180   2 Corinthians 12:9.

181   Psalms 34:17.

182   Psalms 51:17–19.

183   James 4:6-8.

184   Psalms 34:18.

185   Psalms 147:3.

186   2 Corinthians 12:7–8.

187   Isaiah 53:5.

188   1 Peter 4:10.

189   Galatians 1:15.

190   Colossians 4:6.

191   Hebrews 4:16.

192   Ephesians 2:5.

193   Philippians 4:4–5.

194   Proverbs 17:22.

195   Proverbs 14:30.

196   Osteen, Joel. Your Best Life Now: 7 Steps To Living At Your Full Potential. Warner Faith, 154.

197   Ibid, 174.

198   Dobson, James. In the Arms of God. Tyndale House Publishers, 1997.

199   Ibid.

200   1 John 1:9.

201   Ciccarelli, Saundra K. and J. Noland White. Psychology. Third edition, Prentice Hall, 408.

202   Ibid.

203   1 Thessalonians 5:18.

204   Romans 8:14.

Chapter 8: Great Minds

205   1 Corinthians 1:27.

206   Acts 2:38–41.

207   Romans 8:10.

208   Acts 5:41.

209   2 Corinthians 5:14.

210   Williams, Daniel Hale. Biography.com/.rss/full/.

211   "About Dr. Daniel Hale Williams." Biography.com/people/Daniel-hale-williams-9532269.

212   http://provfound.org/index.php/history/history-dr-daniel-hale-williams.

213   "Christine Darden's Biography." History-makers.org/biography/Christine-darden.

214   Darden, Christine. nasa.gov/centers/Langley/news/researchernews/rn_cdarden.html.

215   Ibid.

216   "About Emmett Chappelle." Web.whoi.edu/big/black-history-month-series-2020-emmett-chapelle/.

217   Ibid.

218   "National Inventors Hall of Fame." Invent.org.

219   "About Gladys West." En.wikipedia.org/wiki/sutherland_virginia.

220   Ibid. Livescience.com/amp/30484-best-earth-gravity-map-ever-geoid.html.

221   Ibid. Apnews.com/2dee50a4b3be4564b417f7-f569b38ba.

222   Ibid. Afspc.at.mil/news/article-display/article/1707464/mathematician-inducted-into-space-anc-missiles-pioneers-hall-of-fame/.

223   "About James West." Engineering.jhu.edu/ece/faulty/west-james-e/.

224   Ibid. Cpnas.org/aahp/biographies/james-edward-west.html

225   "About Benjamin Banneker." Math.buffalo.-edu.mad/special/banneker-benjamin.html #abio%20question.

226   Ibid. Haverford.edu/library/news/book-month-

bannekers-almanac.

227   Ibid. Thoughtco.com/Benjamin-banneker-profile-1991360.

228   "Benjamin Banneker Letter to Jefferson." biography.com/.rss/full/.

229   Philippians 2:8.

230   Luke 2:1–20.

231   John 15:13.

232   Matthew 20:28.

233   Isaiah 52:14.

234   1 Peter 2:24.

235   John 3:16.

236   John 3:17.

237   Luke 23:34.

238   1 Corinthians 15:15.

239   Luke 9:35.

240   Mark 2:17.

241   John 5:1–9.

242   Matthew 6:18–20.

243   Hebrews 4:15.

244   John 16:12.

245   Hebrews 12:2.

246   Hebrews 12:1.

247   1 Corinthians 9:24.

248   Psalms 139:14, CBS.

CPSIA information can be obtained
at www.ICGtesting.com
Printed in the USA
BVHW021531210222
629674BV00018B/628